j EASY NF Troupe
Troupe, Thomas Kingsley,
Staying safe at school

7 -19

Staying Safe at School

by **Thomas Kingsley Troupe**

illustrated by **Kat Uno**

PICTURE WINDOW BOOKS
a capstone imprint

Alvaro

Name: **Alvaro**

Birthday: **December 23**

Favorite color: **green**

Favorite food: **spaghetti**

Favorite animal: **shark**

I want to be a: **police officer**

Table of Contents

Staying Safe

Hi! My name is Alvaro. Look at those fire trucks! Don't worry. Everything is OK. We just had a fire drill at my school. All the students and teachers practiced what to do if there were a real fire.

Being at school is a big job. My friends and I are here to learn. And we need a safe place to do that. Come on! Let me show you some ways we stay safe at my school.

On the Bus

For me, staying safe starts early in the morning. I ride a school bus. My friends and I always stay in our seats. Sitting is safer than standing. You never know when the bus might stop suddenly. We try to talk quietly too. We don't want to bother our bus driver. She needs to pay attention to the road.

Later, after school, I'm careful when I get off the bus. I make sure to cross the street in front of the bus's crossing arm. When I do, the driver can see me get to the other side safely.

7

Fire Drills

So what happened when we had our fire drill this morning? First, the fire alarm rang. Our teacher, Ms. Gazda, told us to line up. "No talking, and don't run," she said. She didn't want anyone to fall and get hurt.

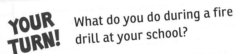

YOUR TURN! What do you do during a fire drill at your school?

8

Everyone in school left the building. The firefighters timed us to see how quickly we got outside. It's good to practice fire drills in case there's a real fire someday.

Watching the Weather

Sometimes we get strong storms where I live. To stay safe at school, we have tornado drills. We pretend a tornado is coming. Some schools have hurricane or earthquake drills too. It depends on where you live.

To practice our drill, everybody goes to a shelter area. It's a place inside the building with thick walls and no windows. We all kneel, facing the wall, bend our bodies to the floor, and cover our heads with our hands. Keeping ourselves tucked like balls helps protect us.

YOUR TURN! What kinds of weather drills does your school have?

Lockdown Practice

All the grown-ups at school want us kids to be safe. They make sure no one's in the building that shouldn't be there. If a dangerous stranger comes to our school, we have a lockdown. During a lockdown, we hide in our classrooms until the police come.

Just like practicing fire and tornado drills, we practice lockdown drills. Ms. Gazda locks our classroom door and turns out the light. We all hide together. Everyone stays quiet. We don't come out until our principal rings the "all clear" bell.

13

14

See It, Say It

Staying safe isn't just about drills. Ms. Gazda says we should watch for ways to stay safe every day. If we see something unsafe or feel unsafe, we should let her know. Maybe there's a spill on the floor, or a chair is broken. Maybe someone is being a bully.

One time I saw Harper pull Daneen's hair—hard. I told Ms. Gazda. She made sure Daneen wasn't hurt. Then she talked with Harper. Bullying is never OK. Everyone needs to feel safe at school.

Lunchroom Rules

Staying safe at lunchtime is important too. When we sit down to eat, we stay put. No running or playing in the lunchroom. We don't share our food either. I sit at a special table for kids who have nut allergies. Certain foods are dangerous for us to eat or touch. The school makes sure we have a safe place to eat our lunch.

YOUR TURN! What does your school do to keep the lunchroom safe for everybody?

Play Smart

We play safe at recess. We wait our turn. No pushing or hitting. No going the wrong way down the slide. And no jumping off the swings! One time Micah jumped off a swing and twisted his foot. George told Ms. Gazda right away, and she came to help. Micah's foot wasn't broken, but he said it really hurt.

A Safe Place

School is a fun place to go. There's lots to do each day. And if we follow the rules, it's easy to learn and stay safe.

Sometimes scary things might happen. But my teacher makes sure my classmates and I are ready for them. Being prepared is how we stay safe at school!

20

Glossary

alarm—a device that makes a loud noise as a warning

allergy—a condition that causes a reaction to something that is harmless to most people, such as foods, pets, or dust

bully—a person who is mean to other people for no reason

dangerous—likely to cause harm

drill—a practiced set of actions

earthquake—a sudden shaking of the ground

hurricane—a strong storm with high winds and rain that starts on the ocean

principal—the head of a public school

protect—to keep safe

recess—a break from schoolwork, usually outside

shelter—a safe, covered place

tornado—a very strong, spinning tube of wind that reaches from the clouds to the ground

Read More

Bloom, Paul. *Rules at Lunch*. The School Rules. New York: Gareth Stevens Publishing, 2016.

Dinmont, Kerry. *Amanda's Fire Drill: A Book About Fire Safety*. My Day Learning Health and Safety. Mankato, Minn.: Childs World, 2017.

Dinmont, Kerry. *Peter's Bus Ride: A Book About Bus Safety*. My Day Learning Health and Safety. Mankato, Minn.: Childs World, 2017.

Internet Sites

Use FactHound to find Internet sites related to this book.

Visit *www.facthound.com*

Just type in 9781515838500 and go.

Critical Thinking Questions

1. How does your school keep you safe?

2. Why is it important for a tornado shelter to have thick walls and no windows?

3. What does "See it, say it" mean to you? Give some examples of unsafe things at school you might tell your teacher about.

Index

Look for all the books in the series:

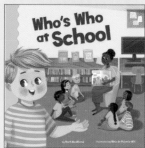

Special thanks to our adviser, Sara Hjelmeland, M.Ed., Kindergarten Teacher, for her expertise.

Editor: Jill Kalz
Designer: Lori Bye
Production Specialist: Laura Manthe
The illustrations in this book were created digitally.

Picture Window Books are published by Capstone
1710 Roe Crest Drive, North Mankato, Minnesota 56003
www.mycapstone.com

Library of Congress Cataloging-in-Publication Data is available on the Library of Congress website.
ISBN: 978-1-5158-3850-0 (library binding)
ISBN: 978-1-5158-4065-7 (paperback)
ISBN: 978-1-5158-3856-2 (eBook PDF)
Summary: How do I stay safe at school? Fire drills, tornado drills, lockdowns . . . School bus safety, playground rules, lunchroom do's and don'ts . . . *Staying Safe at School* defines the many ways school communities keep their members safe, using bright, full-color illustrations and kid-friendly text delivered by a 1st-person student narrator with whom young readers can easily identify.

Shutterstock: jannoon028, (notebook) design element throughout

Printed in the United States of America.
PA49